I LIE ON MY MAT AND PRAY

I LIE ON MY MAT AND PRAY

Prayers by Young Africans

Edited by
FRITZ PAWELZIK

Illustrated by
Georg Lemke

Translated by
Robbins Strong

FRIENDSHIP PRESS • NEW YORK

First published in German under the title
ICH LIEGE AUF MEINER MATTE UND BETE
by Aussaat Verlag, Wuppertal.

Library of Congress Catalog Card No. 64-20103

Copyright 1964 by Friendship Press, Inc.
Printed in the United States of America

CONTENTS

Greetings	vii
I Lie on My Mat and Pray	9
Like a Cool Day between Rainy Seasons	10
Dawn Glistens on the Grasses	13
The Teacher's Prayer: Take My Day in Your Hands	14
The Chief's Prayer: Give Me a Clear Head	15
Bless This Meal	16
The Meal Is Steaming	17
That Was a Good Meal, Lord	18
I Am Not Afraid	19
Is There Work for Me?	20
Waiting for Work	22
Send Us Ships to Takoradi	23
Take Me Safely to Accra	24
There Have Been Bad Accidents	25
No One Can Deceive You	27
You Can Redeem Them	28
When They Are Angry They Need You	29
Your Judgment Is Entirely Different	30

You Are the Leader of Youth	31
Our Country Needs Us	32
We Want to Exercise Our Bodies	34
You Must Teach Us	35
You Are Much Stronger than Juju	36
Despair Grips Me	39
You Are Like the Noonday Sun in the Night	40
Redeem Africa and the Whole World	41
You Have Marked Us for This Continent	42
Let Your Peace Come into This World	44
We Ask for Your Help	45
Lord, We Weep	46
Come, Prepare Us	49
Let Your Spirit Break In	50
Bless Our Brothers in All the World	51
May Our Work Take Place in Your Name	54
Make Us Your People	56
We Are One in Prayer	60
Glossary	61

Greetings

With these prayers, Ghana's young Christians send greetings to young Christians in North America.

What is written here is not a collection of machine-tooled words. You may at times find the words strange, the grammar rough. Perhaps our prayers are not liturgically and dogmatically correct. They spring up like palm trees and cassava roots, like young Christians in their faith. These prayers come out of a full heart, spontaneously; they come now loudly, now softly, just as one speaks to his father.

We pray often for Christians in America. We must stammer out our thanks for the help you have given. We pray for you, pale brothers. We pray for you, darker brothers. But you in mighty America must pray much and persistently for us.

I am happy that I can send these prayers in the name of my friends here. There is only one Master, and we are all brothers.

Fritz Pawelzik

ACCRA
Epiphany 1964

I LIE ON MY MAT AND PRAY

Matthew, Mark, Luke, and John,
four men squat around the mat
on which I lie,
and pray,
and sleep.
Night comes,
sleep comes.
Dear Lord Jesus, come.
Four men
have told us this story.
Your story.
Two sit at the foot,
two at the head.
They will carry me to you,
Lord Jesus Christ,
when the last breath
beats against my tired lips.
Amen.

LIKE A COOL DAY BETWEEN RAINY SEASONS

O Lord, O God,
Creator of our land,
our earth, the trees,
the animals and men,
all is for your honor.
The drums beat it out,
and men sing about it,
and they dance with noisy joy
that you are the Lord.
You have created this glorious,
sun-drenched Africa
and our friends and families and tribes.
You also have pulled the other continents
out of the sea.
What a wonderful world you have made
out of wet mud,
and what beautiful men!
We thank you for all the beauty of this earth.
Everything is like a shining wreath
around your name.
The grace of your creation is like a cool day
between rainy seasons.
We drink in your creation with our eyes.
We listen to the birds' jubilee
with our ears.
How strong and good
and sure your earth smells,
and everything that grows there.
The sky above us
is like a warm, soft Kente cloth,
because you are behind it,
else it would be cold and rough and uncomfortable.
We drink in your creation

and cannot get enough of it.
But in doing this we forget
the evil we have done.
Lord, we call you,
we beg you:
tear us away from our sins
and our death.
This wonderful world fades away.
And one day our eyes snap shut,
and all is over
and dead that is not from you.
We are still slaves of the demons
and the fetishes of this earth,
when we are not saved by you.
Give us radar vision,
that we can see through all the cosmetics
and stage settings of nature
to you.
Bless us.
Bless our land and her people.
Bless our forests with mahogany,
wawa, and cacao.
Bless our fields with cassava and peanuts.
Bless the waters
that flow through our land.
Fill them with fish
and drive great schools of fish
to our seacoast,
so that the fishermen in their unsteady boats
do not need to go out too far.
Be with us youth in our countries,
and in all Africa,
and in the whole world.
Prepare us for the service
that we should render

to our families, the world,
and you.
Grant that youth may know you while young,
so that they may have
a long and happy and wonderful life.
Give us everything in your hour.
Make us ready for every task
that comes from you.
Thus do we praise, honor,
and pray to you,
God the Father, God the Son, and God the Holy Spirit.
Amen.

DAWN GLISTENS ON THE GRASSES

We are awake.
Sleep is still in our eyes,
but at once on our lips
shall be your praise.
We glorify, praise, and adore you.
We—that is, the earth,
the water, and the sky;
that is, the grasses and bushes and trees;
that is, the birds and all the other animals;
that is, the people here on earth.
Everything that you have created
enjoys your sun
and your grace
and becomes warm in it.
Dawn glistens on the grasses.
Mist is still hanging in the trees,
and a soft wind
promises a fine day.
Should we not enjoy everything
that you have created?
We are meant to.
That is why we are so joyful
this dawn,
O Lord.
Grant that the hours and minutes
do not slip away in our hands,
but that we live in your time.
Amen.

THE TEACHER'S PRAYER: TAKE MY DAY IN YOUR HANDS

Wonderful, merciful God,
I put myself in your hands
with the first breath
this morning.
I know you are alive.
I know
your goodness and grace have no end.
I beg you,
heavenly Father,
take my day in your hands.
Push away
all the temptations and wants of this day,
as you push away
threatening storm clouds.
Let me do my work,
let me do it
so that it is good for the boys and girls
and glorifies your name.
Give me right words
and power and love,
so that your image may be rightly painted
for the children in the school.
Let your love and patience
be in everything
I have to teach the children.
May my work be fruitful.
Amen.

THE CHIEF'S PRAYER: GIVE ME A CLEAR HEAD

Now I am sitting here at my desk
and the din of the day is around me
But even here you are Lord,
and I beg you
for your blessing on my work.
Give me strength,
so I can do what must be done.
And may it be good,
not just a hit-or-miss job.
And you know, too,
that decisions must be made today.
They are always very difficult,
and I am dealing with men.
Make plain the right decisions.
Give me a clear head and a warm heart.
And it is always so hard
to issue orders and regulations;
give me your power and humility,
so that they will be rightly issued and received.
Let me never forget
that the workers are my brothers,
that in your eyes they are much more than I am.
They all have families,
honor, feelings, and rights.
Let me never forget
that they are first of all men,
and then workers.
I am sure that when you are with me
my work will succeed
for the welfare of men,
the well-being of my family,
and your glory.
Amen.

BLESS THIS MEAL

Creator Lord,
through whom everything
on this earth grows—
sweet bananas, fat plantains,
sour oranges, dry yams,
rice, corn, and peanuts
from which this good soup is squeezed—
who let the sharp red peppers grow
that keep us healthy
and burn stomachs clean;
who let fresh water burst from the ground,
good, fresh water . . .
Bless for me this meal,
my loving God and Father.
And see to it
that all the atoms are in their right places.
Amen.

THE MEAL IS STEAMING

O Lord,
the meal is steaming before us
and it smells good.
The water is clear and fresh.
We are happy and satisfied.
But now we must think of our sisters and brothers
all over the world
who have nothing to eat
and only little to drink.
Please, please give all of them your food
and your drink.
That is most important.
But give them also
what they need every day
to go through this life.
As you gave food and drink
to the people of Israel in the desert
please give it also
to our hungry and thirsty brothers
now and in all times.
Amen.

THAT WAS A GOOD MEAL, LORD

I thank you, Lord,
that that was such a good meal.
That was a good soup from your peanuts.
That was good meat from your buffaloes.
That was hot pepper and a great yam.
O Lord,
our stomachs are full.
Our bodies have what they need.
That is a new miracle every day.
We thank you for it,
and also for the good taste
that lingers on our tongues.
How refreshing your water was!
With this meal you gave us
the strength required for the day.
Add to it your Spirit
so that we may use it rightly.
Give us, besides food for our bodies,
your heavenly food
for our whole life.
Praised be you, merciful God.
Amen.

I AM NOT AFRAID

The sun has disappeared.
I have switched off the light,
and my wife and children are asleep.
The animals in the forest are full of fear,
and so are the people on their mats.
They prefer the day with your sun
to the night.
But I still know that
your moon is there,
and your eyes
and also your hands.
Thus I am not afraid.
This day again
you led us wonderfully.
Everybody went to his mat
satisfied and full.
Renew us during our sleep,
that in the morning
we may come afresh to our daily jobs.
Be with our brothers far away in Asia
who may be getting up now.
Amen.

IS THERE WORK FOR ME?

The day is there.
There is the sun.
Ships are in the harbor.
But is there work for me?
The others have friends.
They also have money.
They have given
a dash of whiskey.
And I stand aside
and have no work.
Can't you make work for me
in the harbor,
dear Lord,
so that I can share money
with my wife and children?
Then, on Sunday,
I can put something in the plate.
Please, let me have work.
Dear Lord Jesus,
we praise you.
Amen.

WAITING FOR WORK

Here I am, sitting on the wall
waiting for a job.
I count the men,
sitting nearby
waiting for work.
Lord, can't you do something
so that there is more work
and the bosses are more just?
One grows lazy
sitting around.
One gets used to it.
And it hurts me
that once again
I can take nothing home
to my children and wife.
But I will not complain.
I know
you have everything in your hand.
And, just across the street
you let everything grow
so that at least we do not go hungry.
You are a merciful and good God.
What are these wood and clay gods
beside you?
You are the greatest,
and you do as you will.
And that is good for all.
Amen.

SEND US SHIPS TO TAKORADI

Now I am lying here on my mat,
dear God.
The day is over
and there was no work.
Still, I am tired.
And yet
you have given us our daily bread.
And the teacher
lets the children go to school
without paying.
I don't know
what they read and write there.
See to it
that they learn nothing bad.
And please, if it's possible,
let me find work tomorrow;
the children need something to wear.
But I am not grumbling.
Give us all a quiet night
and a sound sleep.
Protect us from the mosquitoes
and see to it that no one is cold.
Send us more ships to Takoradi.
You are a great,
powerful, and loving God.
We praise you
and pray to you.
Amen.

TAKE ME SAFELY TO ACCRA

With you, O Lord,
I will sit in the car
that is taking me to Accra.
The road is now very good,
and the trotros are also better
than the old mammy-trucks.
But because of this the drivers
race like mad along the road.
Guide the driver's foot on the accelerator.
Let him drive slowly
and not become
the murderer of other men.
Let me reach Accra unhurt
and let me carry out my jobs there.
Bring me safely back to my own place,
when it is your will.
Praised be you,
God the Father, God the Son, God the Holy Ghost.
Amen.

THERE HAVE BEEN BAD ACCIDENTS

O Lord, I pray you
for all people who drive machines:
a locomotive, an airplane,
a car, a motorcycle, a scooter.
You know
that these people are often frivolous and tired.
And there have been terrible accidents
that drunks have caused.
How much misery and need
these dead,
these injured,
these knocked-down people
have brought to their families!
Make these drivers more responsible.
Take them to task.
Your word is the only thing
that can change these fellows.
They are deaf and reckless
and show-offs.
You alone can make peace,
even peace on the roads.
Without it everyone
will want to go back to the bush.
And the other people
who use the roads
are school children,
women who are shopping or going to market,
men and other beings
that act like chickens on the road.
How often they are responsible for accidents!
Have these traffic victims prayed?
Have they forgotten
that you are our only savior and helper?

When they have not yet prayed,
or don't know how,
then we ask you,
heavenly Father,
to protect them from accident and danger.
Amen.

NO ONE CAN DECEIVE YOU

Lord, you know
that the buyers and sellers in our land
are very special people.
None of us can deceive you,
neither the buyers,
nor the sellers.
We know
that this is not a laughing matter.
Fraud is too often involved.
Some people hunger,
while others pile up riches.
Let us as buyers and sellers
keep our eyes on that.
We want to pay
what the goods are worth.
But the others
should not take more
than they are worth.
Bring peace there too, O Lord.
Amen.

YOU CAN REDEEM THEM

Criminals, burglars, thieves,
murderers, bandits, street gangsters,
and the like
are not comfortable contemporaries.
O Lord, our eternal Father,
teach these brothers
to leave their evil ways
at once, and turn to you.
How foolish it is to think
that theirs is the quickest way to money,
wealth, and happiness!
They have, I believe, forgotten
that they will be left by the roadside,
when the day of your anger comes,
the awful day,
on which we awake from the dust
to your justice.
They do not know
how terrible you can be to men
who have not done your will,
who have not loved their brothers,
but who, on the contrary, have
robbed, terrorized, attacked,
and murdered them.
You can redeem even these people from evil.
We pray that you will.
Through Jesus Christ we know
how much you love us all.
We pray for your love, O Lord.
Amen.

WHEN THEY ARE ANGRY THEY NEED YOU

We ask you, O Lord,
to say clearly
to workers and bosses
what it means to give and to receive.
Between the two groups
there is lasting misunderstanding.
One wants to receive too much,
the other to give too little.
It sounds so simple,
but it is all very difficult.
And nothing can be done without you.
Press the two partners closer together.
Speak like a father to them.
When one party still refuses to listen,
then be with those who
suffer need.
And when strikes break out,
strikes for justice,
then we ask you
to be by your Spirit
especially among the workers.
Particularly when they are angry
they need you.
We know
we can call upon you for all these things.
This makes us happy and at peace.
Everything is in your hand.
Honor and praise to you,
Holy God.
Amen.

YOUR JUDGMENT IS ENTIRELY DIFFERENT

For judges, defendants, and plaintiffs,
and particularly for barristers,
we pray to you.
How much "palavering" there often is about trifles!
How often formalities rule
and not true law.
Often they have not men in mind
but legal paragraphs.
And none of us can cope with
the cunning of lawyers.
We are grateful
that your judgment is entirely different.
Perhaps it is more severe,
but your grace is there as well.
For that we praise and thank you.
Let the courts of justice
here on earth reflect
your justice and grace.
Amen.

YOU ARE THE LEADER OF YOUTH

We pray, O Lord,
for young people.
For the youth of our land.
For the youth of our church.
It is you who help them grow
in body, mind, and spirit.
We know
they can do nothing without you.
Please, bring these youth
into your manhood.
We nag them continuously.
We constantly find something wrong about them.
And yet they are no worse
than we were.
With age we become ever more proud,
and I am only a few years older than they.
You are the true leader of youth.
You know exactly what they need.
They do not need our musty moralizing.
They do not need our "I know better."
They need your commandments
and your grace.
Give the youth of the world patience,
obedience, humility,
energy, and joy.
We have read
that youth in Europe and America are sad.
Give to them a heart full of gladness.
Let them be your youth,
so that they are not as negative
as we adults;
let them do better than we!
Amen.

OUR COUNTRY NEEDS US

Lord, we pray for ourselves,
for other youth of this country,
for the youth of Africa,
and of the world.
We are awakening,
and we do not know
if we are strong enough
to carry the responsibility
that awaits us.
Our countries are looking to us.
Old men look at us critically.
They scold us and, even worse,
think we are silly.
What then shall we do?
For we are not yet strong enough.
And old men always forget quickly
how weak they were when young.
We have not yet any experience,
and for a long time we shall still not be mature enough
to be leaders.
We come to you.
You understand us.
You have experience with men.
You know what we must do and how.
You can lead us so
that we will be the hope
of our beloved countries.
Help us to contribute our share
to the development of our countries
here in Africa.
We want our Christian Association to play its role,
not because it is ours,
but because you are its Father.

Let us be servants to our countries,
the engine in the car
driving towards a good future,
your future.
Take our complexes from us.
Our country needs us.
Especially the young Christians.
We must play a role in our countries,
your role;
otherwise our countries will go the wrong way.
And we ask you,
let us be good road signs
that we may lead many people to you.
But first of all we must invite them.
And this is what is so difficult.
But with your Spirit
and in your name, everything is possible,
dear Father.
We praise and adore you.
Amen.

WE WANT TO EXERCISE OUR BODIES

Our bodies,
which you have given us,
must be kept healthy
and in good condition.
You know, Lord,
how little we do that.
Our bodies are more like an old beer hall
than your wonderful temple.
Everything in it smells stale,
because we exercise our bodies
and their parts too little.
Now we want to exercise our bodies;
we want to play football.
Loving God,
protect us from accident and danger.
Give us plenty of air in our lungs
and don't let us shout
when someone does not play
the way he should.
May we not play for ourselves,
but for our team.
Let us play fair,
let us play fair,
let us play fair.
We pray especially for this,
hard though it is:
let us so play
that your name
and honor
and goodness
will be praised through our play.
Amen.

YOU MUST TEACH US

Lord God,
Father of Jesus Christ,
you are stronger than all the gods
that live on or under the earth.
There really are not any,
because you are.
The moon is the moon
and no god.
The sun is the sun
and no god.
And the god of our city is not named Takoradi,
but you are God, and your son is Jesus.
Sometimes the fetish priests
do strange things,
but these are only tricks.
And when you are present
no one can be killed by drumming.
You are strong;
stronger than the sea.
And you are high;
higher than the sky.
And then men killed your Son.
That was not good.
But that's the way they are.
We are not any better.
Therefore you must teach us
what we should be.
May I always pray this way,
even when I must go away.
With you I have no more fear.
Amen.

YOU ARE MUCH STRONGER THAN JUJU

You know, dear God,
my people still believe much in juju.
But I don't believe in it any more,
since I believe in you.
But sometimes
I am afraid of it.
Now they are trying again
to get at me with juju.
They want to put
something bad in my head.
They believe in it.
They drum for it,
they dance for it,
and they sing for it.
And I can do nothing about it.
I don't believe in it any more
but I am still afraid of it.
You are much stronger than juju.
Halleluja, Halleluja,
you are my God,
mine, mine, mine.
My great God,
great, great, great.
My strong God,
strong, strong, strong.
My loving God,
loving, loving, loving.
My redeemer, my savior,
my father, father, father.
My hut,
my shadow,
my redeemer, my redeemer, my redeemer.
You are my cave,

my door and my weapon,
when now
evil ones are making juju against me.
But you are still stronger,
much, much stronger.
They are dancing around the drums.
They are making juju against me.
But I will depend entirely on you.
I can do nothing against this juju.
I won't get another fetish priest.
I'll depend only on you.
Even when I am sick
I won't get a fetish priest.
Yes, I have you.
You are always there.
I depend on you.
I thank, thank, thank you.
What is juju against you?
Juju can do nothing
where you are.
Amen.

DESPAIR GRIPS ME

I have no other helper than you,
no other father,
no other redeemer,
no other support.
I pray to you.
Only you can help me.
My present misery
is too great.
Despair grips me,
and I am at my wits' end.
I am sunk in the depths,
and I cannot pull myself up
or out.
If it is your will,
help me out of this misery.
Let me know
that you are stronger
than all misery and all enemies.
O Lord, if I come through this,
please let the experience
contribute to my and my brothers' blessing.
You will not forsake me;
this I know.
Amen.

YOU ARE LIKE THE NOONDAY SUN IN THE NIGHT

O Lord, Creator,
Ruler of the world, Father,
I thank, thank, thank you
that you have brought me through.
How strong the pain was—
but you were stronger.
How deep the fall was—
but you were even deeper.
How dark was the night—
but you were the noonday sun in it.
You are our father,
our mother,
our brother, and our friend.
Your grace has no end,
and your light no snuffer.
We praise you,
we honor you,
and we pray to your holy name.
We thank you
that you rule thus,
and that you are so merciful
with your tired followers.
Praised be you
through our Lord Jesus Christ.
Amen.

REDEEM AFRICA AND THE WHOLE WORLD

Eternal, merciful,
mighty, loving God,
we pray for the strong men of this world.
We think they are very powerful,
and we are afraid of them.
But we also know
that you just laugh at them.
One day you will let them die and all is over.
To us they often seem invincible.
You have handed over to them for a time
part of this world.
Keep them from
sowing discord in their times
or making wars.
Help them to talk less about peace;
but give them a peace-loving heart.
Help them not to promise so much,
but to love men more.
Be also with our leaders here in Africa.
Give them wisdom and patience,
but also strength.
Help us to become a free and redeemed Africa
with truly free people:
free from slavery,
free from fear of men,
free from demons and superstition.
Make us quickly forget
what other people have done to us.
For this we pray humbly,
God the Father, God the Son, and God the Holy Spirit.
Amen.

YOU HAVE MARKED US FOR THIS CONTINENT

O Lord, O Ruler of the world,
O Creator, O Father,
this prayer is for Africa.
For our brothers in the South,
for our brothers in the North.
You know
that the white brothers have made their black brothers
second-class people.
O Lord, this hurts us so much.
We suffer from this.
You have given us a dark skin
so that we may better bear
your strong sun.
Why have our brothers done this to us?
They are not better than we,
and we are not better than they.
What comforts us is
that you always love most
those who suffer most.
We call ourselves Christians on both sides.
But we go to different churches,
as if there were also different heavens.
The white men
still have power in parts of Africa.
Help them to use their power wisely
and accept us as brothers.
Take the mistrust out of their hearts and minds
and make them share with us,
for this is our continent,
or, more truly, yours;
and you have marked us for this continent
and them for the North.
We also pray for ourselves.

O Lord,
keep our hearts free from hatred.
And let us also be grateful for what
missionaries have done here
and others too, for government and for the economy.
Let us become brothers again,
as it should be among your children.
You have died for all,
and risen,
Halleluja!
We praise you, our Father,
who are greater than Europe and Africa;
who love where we hate;
who long ago could have destroyed us.
But you love us so much
and we have not deserved it.
Praise be to you, O Lord!
Amen.

LET YOUR PEACE COME INTO THIS WORLD

O Lord, we pray to you
for peace in this world.
The situation looks desperate,
but you see more than we do.
No one understands another any more.
Everyone knows best.
Everyone wants to force his half-baked ideas
upon other people.
They beat one another,
and they spit at one another,
and they set men,
your children,
against one another.
They build up armaments
and puff themselves up.
They pretend
to have war and peace in their hands.
Show these braggarts
who is Lord of the world,
that you alone can talk
of existence and freedom.
These people know nothing
of what they talk about.
Lord, we ask you
for peace in this world.
Your disobedient children
ask their loving Father for peace.
You are our hope and our peace.
Let your peace come into this world.
Amen.

WE ASK FOR YOUR HELP

Dear Lord, we thank you
that you have brought us salvation
through Jesus Christ, your Son.
We can't thank you enough
for this great gift.
And above all
we must thank you for the peace
that has come into our lives
with our new Lord.
We pray to you for the peace of this world.
We know
that true and lasting peace
can come only from Jesus Christ.
And thus we come to you,
asking for your help
and your peace.
We ask through our Master and Redeemer.
We pray for the rulers of this world.
May they too
find Christ as their personal Savior
and Redeemer.
May they search through all the problems
that torment us today
to find your answer,
the only true one.
We pray
for the Christians of all the world.
Make us your own.
Amen.

LORD, WE WEEP

Lord, we weep
for our brothers in South Africa.
Please hear their cries.
Take the dead into your glory,
and comfort the fallen.
Lord,
South Africa needs your Holy Spirit.
Lord, your children
have been shot.
They have wallowed in their blood
and cried.
Lord, your children
have sat in armored cars
and have shot.
Lord, these are your children.
So are we all.
No one is better than another.
One goes to this church
and the other to that,
but they both pray to you.
One says
that the other is dirty and smells.
And the other says:
give me
what you and your ancestors have built,
because it is on my land.
One of them sleeps in a bungalow
and the other on the ground.
And the hate between them
grows like corn in the rainy season.
Lord you are the peacemaker.
Lord, please, please,
speak with the brothers.

We ask you for this
in the name of our Redeemer, Jesus Christ.
Lord, here are your people.
We want to have a happy evening together,
if you are willing.
We know
that other men are in need and misery
or facing their death.
We pray for them.
You are the master of joy.
Be there with your comfort.
And now, please come to us too,
so that we may really rejoice.
O, come,
merciful, loving, friendly God.
We want now to sing and drum
and be joyful.
In your name we begin.
Amen.

COME, PREPARE US

For your Spirit, holy God,
we pray,
the Spirit
with which you equipped
your prophets,
apostles, martyrs, and confessors,
the Spirit who opens our hearts for your service
as he did theirs.
We seek our brothers,
and find them only
when we open our hearts to them.
We must speak your word to them aright.
They must understand
that you are their Redeemer.
Otherwise they are lost.
Come, Holy Spirit,
prepare us
to enter the huts of others.
Amen.

LET YOUR SPIRIT BREAK IN

On your last days on earth
you promised
to leave us the Holy Spirit
as our present comforter.
We also know
that your Holy Spirit blows over this earth.
But we do not understand him.
Many think
he is only wind or a feeling.
Let your Holy Spirit
break into our lives.
Let him come like blood into our veins,
so that we will be driven
entirely by your will.
Let your Spirit
blow over wealthy Europe and America,
so that men there will be humble.
Let him blow over the poor parts of the world,
so that men there need suffer no more.
Let him blow over Africa,
so that men here may understand
what true freedom is.
There are a thousand voices and spirits
in this world,
but we want to hear only your voice,
and be open only to your Spirit.
Amen.

BLESS OUR BROTHERS IN ALL THE WORLD

Almighty, all loving,
wonderful and great God,
father of our Christian family
that lives all over the world,
we thank you
that today
we can gather in your name.
We are more than two or three.
We are here together
to hear your word,
and we know that you are with us.
We want to love our neighbors.
Give us your Spirit,
so that we may do so.
We love ourselves too much.
At most, perhaps, we love our friends,
and those who now gather with us.
Change that.
Let us see
the other young men in our city:
those loitering around the port,
who fill themselves with palm wine,
who drive heavy trucks,
and who do not observe your laws.
Let us see our brothers
and all those
who suffer want
and all who live across the sea.
You see our brothers thousands of miles away.
You hear how they pray for us.
You see what they do for us.
We want to return to them
what they have given us in your name.

Let us be brothers,
real brothers,
across all boundaries and barriers,
so that the world may see
how your love works.
O Lord, we pray for our brothers:
what hurts them also hurts us,
and hurts you too.
Keep them strong,
well, and in your family;
stand by them in their need and persecution.
We call to you
for our brothers
in South Africa, black and white;
for all our brothers
who carry on your work
in spite of persecution and pain.
Give them your power and your backbone;
so they do not fall.
And they need your Holy Spirit,
so that they do not hate their persecutors
but love them.
Yes, dear Lord,
may we not strike out with words.
Quiet our hearts.
Let us not ask too much for ourselves.
As long as we have shoes on our feet,
let us pray for men who have no feet.
And see to it
that we share with those
who have nothing.
Be the bread of men
who have none.
Be with those
who are suffocated by injustice.

Be with those
who have everything:
big cars, fine houses, and much money.
They are not happier than we.
Be with those
who hunger,
and those
who push away half-eaten plates.
We are all your children.
We need you.
We need your love
so that we can live with one another.
I am so happy
that I can belong to your tribe.
Bless us and our brothers in all the world.
Amen.

MAY OUR WORK TAKE PLACE IN YOUR NAME

O Lord! O God! O Father!
We pray
for all mankind.
We pray that your word
will go deep into the hearts of men,
into each heart.
May the world understand
that there is no God beside you.
That there is no other power than yours.
There are many
who take your word for wind,
and in doing so they think
they are very wise.
But they are fools.
Lord, give them more understanding.
For there are those
who want to do everything themselves.
Please, do not wait
until they collapse.
And there are those
who sleep in church
and also at work.
Get them going.
Please, give power and perseverance to those
who want to help other men.
We pray for all your churches,
for the strong ones and the strange ones.
Give them your Holy Spirit,
so that they do not rely on their liturgies
but on your Spirit.
We pray
for our friends overseas,
who pray and give for us.

Give them your whole, your full blessing.
Please, please, please.
We pray for all organizations
and groups in the world
that seek the welfare of mankind.
You know
that our, your YMCA, is among them.
Give them your power and help.
You know better than we
how our YMCA needs
your help and your blessing
and money from men.
Great tasks lie ahead of us.
Give to us, your YMCA,
wisdom, energy, and love
that we can rightly shoulder
our responsibilty.
O Lord, there is a big job,
but your people are lazy.
There are many
who stand with folded arms
or roll the Kente cloth around their bellies,
but there are few
with dirty hands and callouses.
May our work
take place in your name
and at your command.
Amen.

MAKE US YOUR PEOPLE

O God, we implore you,
bless the men of this land,
this beautiful land,
this green land,
this yellow land
under your wonderful sun.
You know what we need:
food for body, soul, and spirit.
And our land is full of chop.
Full, full, full,
fuller than the big stores.
We thank you for cassava,
which is all along the coast
and grows so fast.
For the fat fish
that do not dive too deep
but come into the nets
of the fishermen of New Takoradi.
We thank you for the yams in the northern region,
for bananas, oranges, and pineapples
that grow everywhere,
and for the fat, green plantains
that we like so much.
You fill our bellies well
and give us power to work and think.
You fill our minds
with wonderful pictures of the sea,
of the forests, and of men.
You have given us food
for souls,
and thus for all
that **we are.**
You have given us

your Son,
the Lord Jesus Christ,
who gives us eternal life.
Body, soul, and spirit are filled by you.
We ask you this,
because it is important
for all people
who have something to say in this land.
Be with those who are politicians.
Be with the chiefs
who lead our families and tribes.
They should be servants
as your Son was,
they should not look out for themselves.
They should not fill their pockets with money,
or their heads with pride.
You are directing them aright,
we depend entirely on you.
And you see
what is happening
in Alabama, in South Africa,
and elsewhere in the world.
Your children do not understand each other
because they have different skins.
But the heart, the soul,
and everything under the skin
is the same.
You have made us dark,
because the sun is so hot and burning here.
You did not want to mock us.
And here, one feels he is somebody,
because he belongs to the party or the tribe.
O God, unite all men.
Unite our small world here in Ghana
with its chiefs and parties,

and the great world with its bombs and big armies.
Come, O merciful God,
with your Holy Spirit, to our land.
Make us your people,
that we may serve
with hearts and hands.
And we ask all this of you
in the name of our Lord Jesus Christ
who died and rose for us.
Amen.

WE ARE ONE IN PRAYER

O Lord, our heavenly Father,
You hear us praying here in Takoradi.
You hear our brothers praying in Africa,
in Asia, in Australia,
in America, and in Europe.
We are all one in prayer.
We praise and honor you,
and we beg you
that we may rightly carry out your commission:
to witness and to love,
in our church and throughout the whole world.
Accept our prayers graciously,
even when they are somewhat strange.
We praise you and pray to you
through Jesus Christ, our Lord.
Amen.

GLOSSARY

cassava	A plant whose starchy roots are a basic food, from which tapioca is made.
chop	Food.
dash	A tip; gift; bribe (colloquial — both verb and noun).
juju	Witchcraft; casting of spells; the art of the medicine man often practiced with drumming, fetishes, taking of oaths and prayers.
Kente cloth	Local handwoven cloth with bright patterns. Used as the national costume of Ghana.
mammy-truck	An open truck fitted with benches for transport of passengers as well as goods. Sometimes decorated with colorful slogans of a religious nature.
trotro	A small bus.
wawa	An African soft wood.

THOSE WHO PRAYED:

Edward K. Amuah
18 years old, student
Takoradi youth leader

C.C. Bekoe-Tabiri
Senior Civil Servant, Sekondi-Takoradi
President of the YMCA of Takoradi

Tobbe Ewe
Takoradi

John Grunshie
Porter, Takoradi-Effia-Kuma

Samuel Obeng
20 years old, rector of a people's school, Takoradi
Recording secretary, YMCA, Takoradi

Sam Oni
Student, Sekondi-Takoradi
Hi-Y president

Fritz Pawelzik
YMCA Fraternal Secretary
Takoradi

Kofi Quanstson
Teacher, Takoradi

Fritz Pawelzik, who collected and originally translated into German these prayers by young Ghanaians, is a YMCA fraternal secretary in Ghana. He is German, married to a Finnish wife, and has two daughters. He has worked extensively both with students and with dock workers in Takoradi, the port city of western Ghana, and now lives in Accra, the capital of the country.

He has written a novel about an African student and is working on two other books with an African background.

Redesigned by Louise E. Jefferson